★AMERICA THE BEAUTIFUL

Illustrated by Stacy Venturi-Pickett

ideals children's books.
NASHVILLE, TENNESSEE

ISBN 0-8249-5504-8

Copyright © 2005 by Ideals Publications

Printed and bound in the U.S.A.

The Statue of Liberty reminds us of America's freedom.

The White House is the home of the president and his family.

America's laws are made in the United States Capitol.

The Washington Monument was named for George
Washington and is over 550 feet tall.

The National Archives Building houses
important historic documents.

The Liberty Bell is in Philadelphia, Pennsylvania. Because
it has a crack, it can no longer be rung.

The Gateway Arch was built in St. Louis, Missouri, in 1965.

The FBI (Federal Bureau of Investigation) building
is in Washington, D.C.

George Washington was America's first president.

Mount Vernon, in Alexandria, Virginia, was the home of George Washington.

Monticello was the home of Thomas Jefferson, the third president of the United States.

The Jefferson Memorial is in Washington, D.C.,
and was named for Thomas Jefferson.

Air Force One is the name of the president's jet.

The president's helicopter is called *Marine One*.

The Lincoln Memorial reminds people of Abraham Lincoln and his presidency.

Inside the Lincoln Memorial, there is a large statue of President Lincoln.

Arlington House was the home of Robert E. Lee,
a great American general.

The Tomb of the Unknowns reminds visitors of the soldiers who have died for America's freedom.

The Franklin D. Roosevelt Memorial includes a statue of his dog, a Scottish Terrier named Fala.

The National World War II Memorial is in Washington, D.C.

The faces of presidents Washington, Jefferson, Roosevelt, and Lincoln were carved into Mount Rushmore.

The U.S. Marine Corps War Memorial, in Washington, D.C., honors Marines who fought for our country.

The John F. Kennedy Eternal Flame is in Arlington National Cemetery and always stays lit.

The John F. Kennedy Center for the Performing Arts
is in Washington, D.C.

The Korean War Veterans Memorial is located
in Washington, D.C.

The Vietnam Veterans Memorial contains the names
of soldiers who died in the Vietnam War.

The Old Post Office Pavilion is now more like a shopping mall.

The Library of Congress is the largest library in the world.

In the Supreme Court Building, the United States justices make their decisions.

Union Station is not only a train station in Washington, D.C., but also has many shops and restaurants.

America's dollar bills are printed at the Bureau of Engraving and Printing.

The United States one-dollar bill features a picture
of George Washington.

"The Metro" is the nickname for Washington, D.C.'s subway system.

The Golden Gate Bridge is in San Francisco, California, and is over one mile long.

A bronze statue of scientist Albert Einstein sits outside
the National Academy of Sciences building.

One of the Smithsonian museum buildings
is called "The Castle."

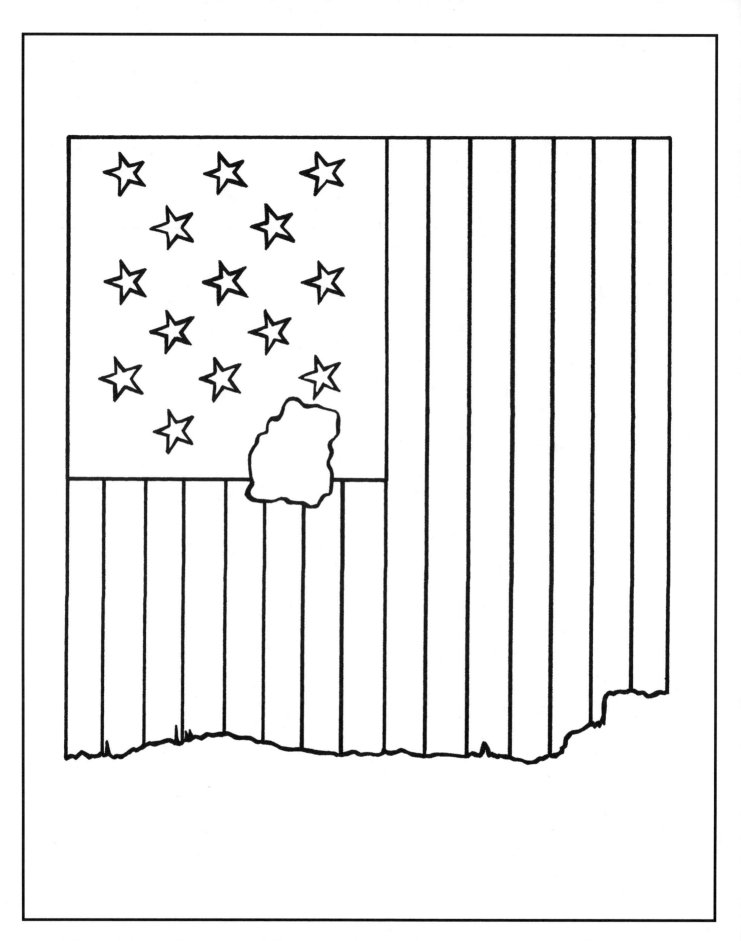

The Star-Spangled Banner is in the Smithsonian National
Museum of American History in Washington, D.C.

Dorothy's "ruby slippers" and Lincoln's hat are in the National Museum of American History.

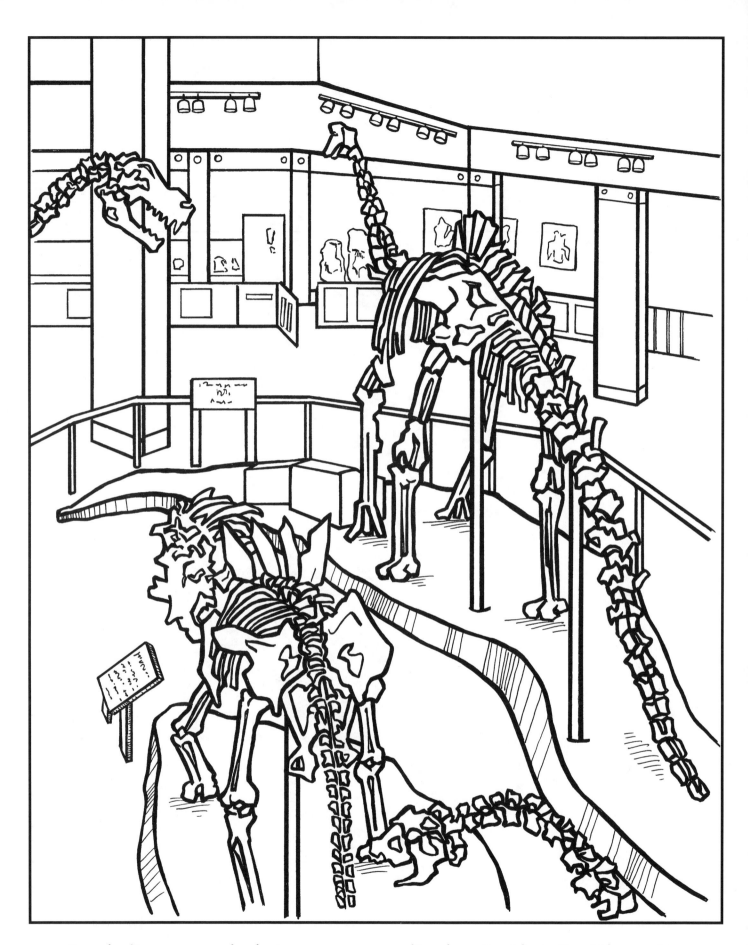

Real dinosaur skeletons are on display in the Smithsonian
National Museum of Natural History in Washington, D.C.

The giant pandas at the National Zoo, in Washington, D.C.,
came to America from China.

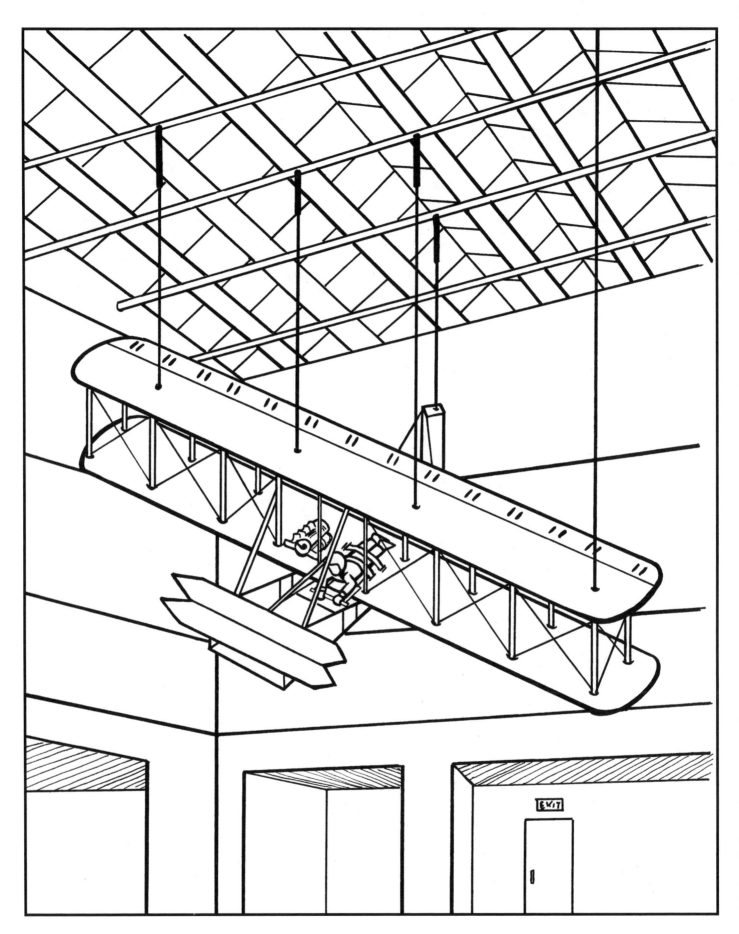

The Wright Brothers' plane *Flyer One* is in the
Smithsonian National Air and Space Museum.

The Pentagon is the headquarters for the United States
Department of Defense.

The National Cathedral is in Washington, D.C.

St. John's Episcopal Church is across the street
from the White House in Washington, D.C.

These men are dressed like colonial soldiers
from the Revolutionary War.

Cherry trees bloom in the springtime along the Potomac River.

Draw your own patriotic picture here!